P9-BIR-201

ST. HELENA PUBLIC LIBRARY
1492 LIBRARY LANE
ST. HELENA, CA 94574-1143
(707) 963-5244

10/12 ST. HELENA LIBRARY

Crafty Kids

How to make a Mask

Paul Humphrey

Photography by Chris Fairclough

SEA-TO-SEA
Mankato Collingwood London

ST. HELENA LIBRARY

This edition first published in 2008 by
Sea-to-Sea Publications
1980 Lookout Drive
North Mankato
Minnesota 56003

Copyright © Sea to Sea Publications 2008

Printed in China

All rights reserved.

Library of Congress Cataloging-in-Publication Data

Humphrey, Paul, 1952-
　　How to make a mask / by Paul Humphrey.
　　　　p.cm. (Crafty kids)
　　ISBN 978-1-59771-101-2
　　　1. Masks--Juvenile literature. 2. Paper work--Juvenile literature. I. Title.

TT898.H86 2007
736.98--dc22

2007060718

9 8 7 6 5 4 3 2

Published by arrangement with the Watts Publishing Group Ltd, London.

Planning and production by Discovery Books Limited
Editor: Rachel Tisdale
Designer: Ian Winton
Photography: Chris Fairclough
Series advisors: Diana Bentley MA and Dee Reid MA,
Fellows of Oxford Brookes University

The author, packager, and publisher would like to thank the following
people for their participation in this book: Auriel and Ottilie Austin-Baker.

Contents

What you need 4

Marking the eyes 6

Cutting the eyes 8

Making the mouth 10

Painting the eyes and mouth 12

Making the hat and bow tie 14

Making the hair 16

Fixing the hat and bow tie 18

Making the nose 20

Wearing your mask 22

Steps 24

What you need

Do you like clowns?
Here's how to make a
clown mask.

These are
the things
you will need:

A large
paper plate

An eraser

A pencil

Colored card stock

A felt-tip pen

4

Safety scissors

White glue

Paints and paint brushes

Sticky tabs

A colored table tennis ball

Raffia

A long piece of elastic

Adhesive tape

Wool

5

Marking the eyes

First, paint the paper plate white.

Hold the plate against your face. Feel where your eyes are.

Ask a friend to mark
where your
eyes are with
a felt-tip pen.

Cutting out the eyes

Draw circles on the paper plate where your eyes are.

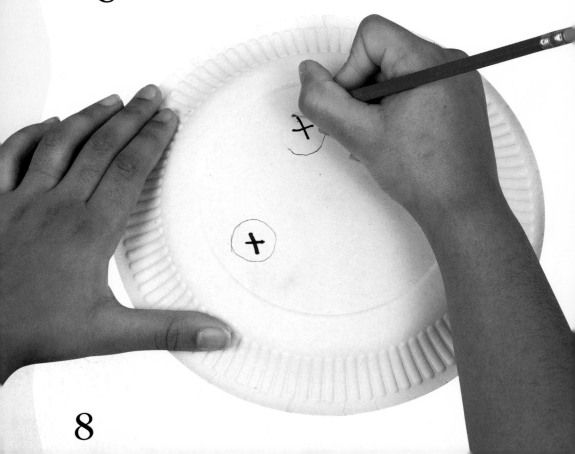

Then cut
out the
circles.

Making the mouth

Now ask a friend to draw where your mouth is.

Fold the plate in half and cut out the mouth across the fold.

Painting the eyes and mouth

Next, paint around the eye holes in bright colors.

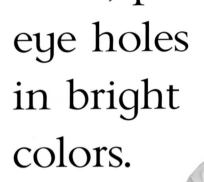

Paint smiling lips
around the mouth.

Making the hat and bow tie

Cut out a hat and bow tie from the card.

Decorate them
with strips of
card. Attach
raffia to the
hat with
tape.

15

Making the hair

Cut the
wool
into
strands.

Glue the wool to each
side of the mask to
make hair.

17

Fixing the hat and bow tie

Use sticky tabs to stick the hat and bow tie onto the mask.

Making the nose

To make the nose, press on the table tennis ball to make a flat edge.

Then use sticky tabs
to stick the ball onto
the mask.

Wearing your mask

Use the pencil and eraser to make a hole on each side of the mask.

Thread the elastic through each hole.

22

Finally, tie
a knot in
each end.

Now
you can
wear your
mask!

Steps

Can you remember all of the steps to make your mask?

1. Mark and cut out the eyes.

2. Mark and cut out the mouth.

3. Paint the eyes and mouth.

4. Make the hat and bow tie.

5. Make and glue the hair.

6. Attach the hat and bow tie.

7. Make and attach the nose.

8. Tie elastic.

9. Wearing your finished mask.

24